"F"

Failed
in the
School of
Love

Briandt I. Gokah

COPYRIGHT Braiandt I. Gokah

FAILED IN THE SCHOOL OF LOVE.

ISBN: 978-978-55454-4-9

PUBLISHED IN THE FEDERAL REPUBLIC OF NIGERIA BY:
Aaron & Hur Publishing (A member of the BSA Group)
16, Thomas Salako Street, Ogba-Ikeja, Lagos, Nigeria
Tel: 07035121346, 08097032664
E: info@aaronandhurpublishing.com
W: www.aaronandhurpublishing.com

Author's Contact
BRAINDT I. GOKAH
+265 992 701 811
E-mail: isaacb.gokah@gmail.com
P.O. BOX 30366 LILONGWE 3 MALAWI

Dedication

First and foremost, to the Holy Spirit for granting me the grace to unearth this hidden gift in me and the inspiration to write this book. I ask for His continues grace to manage this gift and to fulfill the dominion mandate of being fruitful and multiply and manage every increase for the fulfilment of His purpose of my life.

To my beautiful wife, kids and to my Mum, who have supported me and inspired me to become who I am today.

To my late Dad, Dickson Worlanyo Drah-Goka, whose life taught me how to impact others through whatever I have, no matter the size.

And, to Bishop Solomon Adebayo who taught me the scriptures and how to read books and to write one.

Contents

Introduction

I have failed in the school of Love. Many have failed in the school of LOVE. Actually, the whole world has failed in the school of love. Never has the world witnessed reference to love as it is today but at the same time the world has also never witnessed hatred in the measure we see it today. Crime, strife, brutal murder and war are clear indication of a society that has lost it all in the pursuit of love. The fabric of every society is built with the chords of love. Whether you are black or white, Christian or Buddhist, the subject of love is indisputably the foundational value for all people and race.

Love is certainly not a feeling but it makes you feel!

In modern society, technological advancement in the area of movies has reduced the value of love to a mere feeling. Love is certainly not a feeling but it makes you feel! Yes, love is expressible! Most people have misunderstood love to mean a mere conjecture of feeling for one another. That is emotion and a product of the soul. Love is more than that. Love is a product of the spirit man! Love requires you to even love your enemy. In fact, for Christians, Jesus put it this way that if love is just give-and-take, that is, if you love me I will love you back, then even non-believers are good at it than Christians.

Love is certainly not when things are rosary. The bible says love covers multitude of sins. You see, that is why the world does not understand this, that one person died on the cross to wipe out everyone else's sin – just like that! It is all about love. Love covers your weakness. Love is not pompous! Love does not keep record of wrongs done to it. Most of us have understood love to mean only when one expresses an emotion towards you in hugging or in a kiss. However, love is more than this! You see, most of us have understood love from its expression but not from its source and so have missed its essence altogether.

Now, we need to get this once and for all. You see, the Bible says that God created us in His own image according to Genesis 1:26. Then, in 1 John 4:8 the Bible says that "Anyone who does not love does not know God, because God is love". No human being is created in the image of Satan but Satan is able to possess a man. Satan does not have the ability to love. He fakes it. That is why we have a lot of fake love all around us. I love you today and by tomorrow I hate you. A boy tells a girl I love you with all my heart today but by tomorrow, he says I regret marrying you. Anyone who gets love from Satan would definitely live to regret it. It reminds me about those Nigerian movies we often watch where people go for love charms. I tell you, that is not just fiction but a reflection of reality. I have grown up in a village where that is common. The charm often works but when it is over, the hatred it generates is like an unquenchable wild fire.

Let me tell you my little secret. There is this one I was introduced to that I did but it didn't work. There is a flower commonly referred to as a love flower that grows in farms. The charm is that you would weed beneath the flower along the path and place a coin under it. It is said that when the lady you intend it for sees it, she would forever run after you. I did this but it never worked. That girl was never my friend until I left the village.

Every human being is created in the image of God and has the image of God called love. The nature of God is in us. The gene of God is in us. God sheds His love into our hearts through the Holy Spirit (Romans 5:5). There are three positive forces that controls the world i.e. faith, hope, and love but the Bible says the greatest of these three is love (1 Corinthians 13:13).

Just take a minute and think through this: if everyone has been created in the image of God and has taken on the virtue of love, then why is it that hatred and strife have consumed the very fabric of our current society so much. Secondly, the world's understanding of love is what is most found in marriages, why then do husbands and wives fight, probably the most? Better still, why is it that fighting is most common between couples? Hear this, God is spirit and His love is Spirit. It can only take the spiritually discerning to grasp what is going on in our societies. Satan is also spirit, I hope you know that? Satan is the counterfeit of God. His main mission is to portray himself as God almighty but know this, an orange tree cannot bear mango fruits. He has confused many people as to believing what is right or wrong but when what he has handed down to men begins to bear fruits, his true nature begins to emerge. That is why you don't have to be surprised, when one individual or a group of people believe that the only way to demonstrate their love to their god or in what they believe in is to shoot down a plane carrying innocent people or blow up a place. Love is not destructive, it builds up.

Most importantly, the answer to those quest‑ions can be found in Romans 1:18-32:

> *For the wrath of God is revealed from heaven against all ungodliness and wickedness of men who by their wickedness suppress the truth. For what can be known about God is plain to them, because God has shown it to them.*
>
> *Ever since the creation of the world his invisible nature, namely, his eternal power and deity, has been clearly perceived in the things that have been made. So they are without excuse; for although they knew God they did not honor him as God or give thanks to him, but they became futile in their thinking and their senseless minds were darkened.*
>
> *Claiming to be wise, they became fools, and exchanged the glory of the*

immortal God for images resembling mortal man or birds or animals or reptiles. Therefore, God gave them up in the lusts of their hearts to impurity, to the dishonoring of their bodies among themselves, because they exchanged the truth about God for a lie and worshiped and served the creature rather than the Creator, who is blessed for ever! Amen.

For this reason God gave them up to dishonorable passions. Their women exchanged natural relations for unnatural, and the men likewise gave up natural relations with women and were consumed with passion for one another, men committing shameless acts with men and receiving in their own persons the due penalty for their error.

And since they did not see fit to acknowledge God, God gave them up to a base mind and to improper conduct. They were filled with all manner of wickedness, evil, covetousness, malice. Full of envy, murder, strife, deceit, malignity, they are gossips, slanderers, haters of God, insolent, haughty, boastful, inventors of evil, disobedient to parents, foolish, faithless, heartless, ruthless. Though they know God's decree that those who do such things deserve to die, they not only do them but approve those who practice them. (RSV)

As from old, due to the disobedience of men, God gave the human race up to a debased (corrupted, degraded) mind to do what ought not to be done. That is why true love is scarcely found anywhere in the world today. Men have simply resorted to all manner of evil. It started a long time ago and now it is at a modernized or technological stage. Paul said they have resorted to all manner of wickedness, evil, covetousness, malice. Full of envy, murder, strife, deceit, malignity, they are gossips, slanderers, haters of God, insolent, haughty, boastful, inventors of evil, disobedient to parents, foolish, faithless, heartless, and ruthless. No love, because love does not condone any of these.

1

The Supreme Definition of Love

Love is a virtue. It is simply an attitude. Love has many colours, faces, and shapes. You can find it in every situation of life.

Love is a virtue. It is simply an attitude. Love is an inner force that controls a person on the outside. I know you were expecting me to quote that 'supreme' definition of love. Unfortunately, there is no such thing as the definition of love! Love has many colours! Of course many have tried to coin their own definition of love. Just try asking three people separately and you would find out what each of them believes or understands as love. However, there is a supreme 'characterization' or 'attribution' of love by the Supreme Creator of the universe, God. He said, in the Holy Bible, 1Corinthians 13: 4-8:

> *"Love is patient, Love is kind. It does not envy, it does not boast, it is not proud. It is not rude, it is not self-seeking, it is not easily angered, it keeps no record of wrongs. Love does not delight in evil but rejoices with the truth. It always protects, always trusts, always hopes, always perseveres. Love never fails..."*

Aren't all these virtues and attitudes? The above characterisation of love tells us that love is far more than what we proclaim with our lips everyday – ***I love you***! Can you persevere/endure in patience, hope and trust always? How many times have you said to someone that I love you but sooner or later that relationship ended? But love NEVER FAILS! Love is not emotions. It is not about the romance of buying flowers or lighting up candles or taking your partner for a cozy dinner! That's human love, not love from above. Love has many colours, faces, and shapes. You can find it in every situations of life. How many of us can still buy a rose for our loved one even when he/she angers us? **But love is giving and giving to the undeserving**. This book is about provoking your thought on the understanding of who you are – created in God's own image. God is love, so you ought to be love too!

Let's take the above attributions one by one.

Love is patient

How long can you tolerate your nagging wife? How long can you tolerate an insensitive husband? Well, these are calls to love – patience, hope and trust that it would be well! It is said that "show me your friend and I will tell you your character" If you truly love me, then you definitely would have the patience for my odds!

Now, one common statements people make is this: I have been patient with you enough! However, let me ask you my friend; how long have you being patient with yourself? Will you reject yourself for the wrongs you have inflicted on others? If not, why do it to others? Remember, the thumb rule is this; "do it to others as unto yourself!"

Have you ever come across someone who everybody knows to be very wicked? It is often said that the good people do not live long but rather wicked people live long. My friend, this is how patient God is! The Bible says God does not rejoice in the destruction of the unrighteous. Let me open your eyes to something. I have witnessed people who serve voodoos (idols) and die instantly because they have not obeyed one command by the charm. Now let me ask you if you are a Christian, how many times have you sinned in the secret and have continued to live? I can tell you honestly the number of times I have personally looked over my shoulders when I find myself doing something that I know God will never approve of. I know definitely if that were Satan, he would have killed me right there. Satan does not have love in him so he is not patient. God is love, so He is patient with all of us.

Imagine if the world is patient! We will not be discussing issues such as drugs trade, coup de tats, prostitutions, armed robbery, etc. Patience tolerates people's weaknesses and shortcomings. Patience believes in hope and trust that hard work will certainly bring rewards.

Love is kind

Probably, this is the most common one the world understands as love. Kindness as in gifts and roses! Most Ladies are dead to this, "if he loves me he would take care of me". He would not withhold so and so from me. You see love is not selfish, love shows kindness. Love believes that what is good for him is good for his/her love one too. Listen that is why the new commandment that Jesus gave stipulates that you should love your neighbour as yourself.

Love does not envy

Look at this scripture: Matthew 22:39 says "...*Thou shalt love thy neighbour as thyself*" Have you ever been envious of yourself? Love says what my neighbour has is as good as I have it, so would I envy? Hatred says what my neighbour has is not mine, it makes him look better than me, so I must have it. If love dwells in you, you would be happy for the next person for what God has packaged him with, you wouldn't envy him. Envies have destroyed so many relationships. Wives and husbands envious of each other's' possession or status!

Love does not envy. Just the way you would feel having it, feel the same way for your neighbour as well. Envy and covetousness has driven crimes in our societies. Everyone is specially packaged with his/her goodies but many people want to have things they are not packaged with or are not prepared for.

Love does not boast and is not proud (Humility)

Love sees itself as good as the other. Love does not see itself more highly than others. Love is simply humble and does not exalt itself above others. Pride drives unforgiveness. Pride is simply a sign that someone does not love you, period! Love sees everyone else as himself. That is why the second and greatest commandment, according to Jesus, is to love your neighbour as yourself. Pride is seeing yourself better than others. Another word for boasting is pretension – i.e. self-importance. Love sees itself equally important as the other but not more important as the other.

Love is not rude

Love is not disrespectful, impolite, offensive or ill-mannered. Rudeness, and its synonyms does not make its victim feel good, it hurts. If you love someone as yourself, just as any of these attitudes would hurt you, you don't use it on that person. Many men have failed in this area. They treat their wives as second-class human being. They simply think their wives do not have an opinion or say in anything. Oh, many Ladies have failed in this area as well. They are ill-mannered or rude towards their men even in public.

Love is not self-seeking

Love is not selfish. Love wants the same for others as he has. I have failed and so have many failed in this pursuit. Jesus did not make a mistake when He said that the second greatest commandment is to love your neighbour as yourself. That's the trait of love. Your closest person is your partner. Love places above everyone else or at minimum, just at par as itself.

It is completely contradictory to love someone as yourself and at the same time place yourself first. Lovers think or focus more on others than themselves. It doesn't mean thinking less of themselves but thinking of themselves less. Love is simply selfless.

Love is not easily angered

Love gets angry, even God does. Don't be too religious or too polite about it, expect it! I read this account in Exodus 32, particularly versus 10, when God asked Moses to leave Him alone because He was angry. So if God can be angry, don't fool yourself. But the truth is this, do not get angry easily. One of the attributes of love is self-restraints or self-control. Anger can be mastered or controlled. Love is not **"easily"** angered. That means lovers may get angry but that anger should not be triggered by any mere situation. A lover should not be found getting angry at everything.

Love keeps no record of wrongs done to it

> *Hatred stirs up quarrels but love covers all sins*
> *Proverbs 10:12*

Note, it doesn't mean that those who are in love do not have disagreements. Actually, that is what defines love. Let me tell you something which might surprise you. In my marriage, disagreements started as early as the first week after our wedding. However, it was not also too long when both of us realised that it's our disagreements that strengthens us. We had recognized that even though our disagreements are often fierce, we always find that internal conviction and peace to forgive each other so easily. We often brea k down in tears and forgive each other and tell ourselves nothing can separate us.

Forgiveness is a true character of Love. God showed it Himself. We were still sinners when Jesus died for us. Remember: forgiveness is tic-for-tac. "Father forgive us as we forgive those who trespass against us" Forgiveness is a give-and-take!

Most often when people have been advised, they don't see its value until they find themselves in similar situations. It was our several disagreements that my wife and I remembered a wise counsel we received in the course of our lives. It took me and my wife over five years to realize this. In any true love relationship, it is your non-coercive ability to overcome the effects of disagreements, which defines your love for each other. No love relationship is disagreement-free. If there is one, watch out the day a disagreement would break out, the collapse of that relationship will be great!

It is the misconception about how a love relationship should be or the misunderstanding of how lovers should behave that sets the scene for disappointments in most relationships. It is our assumption about how perfect lovers should be that misleads us. No man/woman is perfect! I thought you loved me? How can you say you love me and behave like this? You see, it is the assumptions we make about the character of love that deceives us and break our hearts. That is why it's said "love has many colours". Locate yours within God's given characteristics! Stop assuming what love is in your partner. It will soon hurt you if you find out sooner or later the colour of your lover's love!

You cannot love without having the heart to forgive and you know the "bad" news is that you would have to forgive all your life! Jesus said offenses would come. So get over it. Forgiveness is the character of true lovers! Jesus provided the best answer regarding this. He said to his disciples, who asked Him how many times they should forgive those who offend them, that they should forgive 70 times 7 (Matt. 18:21-22) which totals 490 times. How many of us have managed to forgive our partners even 100 times before we give up? Anyone who claims to love you but cannot forgive you does not love you! Don't waste your time on him/her! Love is tolerant!

Take note of this, forgiveness is not premeditative, neither is it a contract. That's, it should not be like we have agreed to forgive each other. That would be a sign of artificial love. Forgiveness comes from within. It's our nature. You know, God is love and that is His nature. Forgiveness is a character of love. So it must not be forced or arranged. It has to flow naturally. Have you ever witnessed a dispute settlement where the parties were asked to shake hands as a sign of forgiveness but they go their ways without really forgiving each other? Have you also heard about couples that fight over and over again but cannot be persuaded to separate by their family and friends? What do you think is the difference between these two scenarios? It's the natural forgiveness!

Love forgives. Love does not keep record of wrongs done to it. Because God is love, He does not keep record of wrongs of those who he has saved. That is why He can use just anybody whether he/she is a murderer or armed robber without reminding him/her or showing him/her records of the past. God is love, so His mercy never comes to an end! Love covers multitudes of sin!

Love does not delight in evil but rejoices with the truth

You see, no evil survives under the sun. So if you love someone you would not want to allow that one to be destroyed. Because the ultimate end of evil is destruction. Love will always be happy with the truth and eschew evil. God is love and God is truth. You cannot separate love from truth. Everyone who loves also wishes you well. That is why the Bible says a father who loves his child disciplines him. The truth always stands! You know lies destroy. So if you are rejoicing with someone in evil, you are simply helping the person to destruction. If you love someone, you will not help him/her to self-destruction.

Love always protects

A synonym for love is care. What you care about you protect. You cannot claim to love something and wouldn't care about it. God loved the world and showed He cares for it. That's why He was willing to send His only son to die to save it. Naturally, no person, especially women, would be inclined that you love him/her without you defending them. Protection also means shielding. Love covers or shields our shortcomings. No true lover will expose your shortcomings to the world. If your lover is found of telling everyone how bad you're then it is likely that he/she doesn't love you or probably he/she has failed in love.

Love always trusts and Hopes

Many say that love is based on trust. Correct! But do you really know what trust means? So many people I have heard talked above trust presume that it is something that must be earned, but let me surprise you, trust in the school of love is not earned. Words for trust is synonymous to hope. Trust also means faith, hope, expectation, belief, etc. These are not tangible things or things that are based on past experiences. Yes, your trust can be boosted by past result but is basically faith – the unseen. Hope, I believe is the strongest force that keeps relationships. The moment you have hope, you have a lifeline for your relationship. It will keep you going without you being tired. You just believe that your partner will get better or give his/her best.

Love always perseveres

Endurance is required of every lover. No true lover quits! It is expected of every lover to have patience because the person you are engaging in a relationship is not you, so don't expect him/her to act just like you. Take your time to understand him/her. This would require perseverance.

Love never fails

Lastly, my friends, I didn't write this book at the time when all is rosy in my marriage. That is, I was not the master of these characteristics of love. Rather, it was the challenges that I had in my marriage that inspired me to find out what love really is and I can tell you confidently that this is the only singular reason why my marriage still exists today. True love never fails because the author and originator of love, never fails. Our God never fails. No love that is based on the solid word of God can fail. You see, the love of God makes you love your spouse as yourself. Therefore, as much as you never want to fail, so you will not allow your spouse to fail as well.

2

The NEW Commandment

L ove is a command and not a choice. Most of us are very familiar with the Ten Commandments that Moses received from God but have no idea about the NEW commandment Jesus gave. Jesus said "A new commandment I give unto you, that ye love one another; as I have loved you, that ye also love one another. By this shall all men know that ye are my disciples, if ye have love one another." (John 13:34-35). Jesus called it the royal law (James 2:8). Then a Pharisees lawyer asked Him, which is the greatest commandment in the law? Jesus answered him and said:

> *"... "You shall love the LORD your God with all your heart, with all your soul, and with all your mind. This is the first and great commandment. And the second is like it: You shall love your neighbor as yourself. On these two commandments hang all the Law and the Prophets. ""*
>
> *(Mt 22:37-40, NKJV)*

Jesus did not miss words at all; neither did he contradict the Ten Commandments. He said; first, love God your creator with your all. Then second, love His creation. God's commandment about relationship is simple – "Love your neighbour as yourself"! Who is your closest neighbour? If you are still living under your parent's roof, your closest neighbour is your parents and siblings. Look at this scripture: 'Honor your father and your mother,' and, 'you shall love your neighbor as yourself.' (Matthew 19:19, NKJV). The first closest neighbour to everyone born under the sun is a parent. Love must start from there. Imagine if every parent truly understands love and have rigorously taught his children, just as he/she did for how to talk or walk, how the world would have been. I bet you that the world would have been a peaceful place always. Note, loving your parents honours them. It is undisputable in every society or religion that any son or daughter who does not honour the parent is considered as not loving them.

For those who have graduated from their parents' homes, your closest neighbour may not be your father or mother but probably your spouse or girl/boyfriend or your friends or your next house neighbour. When you are married, God adds this simple layer of command to the above:

> **Woman humble yourself to your husband; Man "Love" your wife**

God instructed man to love the wife but only asked the wife to humble herself to the husband. By this instruction, it seems and many have argued so, that love is required of men only or more of men than women in relationships. By this proposition, it means men needs to love double or twice as much as is required of women. However, as you would realise later in this book, "humility" is a character of "love". I tell you that this command is not different from the first but just a matter of emphasis. Notice, the commandment about love is to ALL irrespective of your gender, race or ethnicity. It didn't say "men love your neighbour" but rather whoever you are, love your neighbour. So simply; woman, love your neighbour; man, love your neighbour! Who is the closed neighbour to a wife or a husband than the husband and wife respectively? In earthly relationships, love is expressed mostly between a man and woman. So loving your neighbour could mean showing love to your spouse and not a requirement for men only! As pointed out earlier, interestingly, humility is a character of love – love is not boastful or proud!

But wait a minute, did God see this coming and hence the specific emphasis? Woman, be humble and man love her. I have been young and now I am old – to borrow some few words from King David. The most common problem I have heard and seen of women in marriage is about humility. Am I right? Also, about men is that of not showing love. Am I right on this one too? Man, can you continue to stay with a nagging woman. How do you handle a woman who thinks she knows it all or she is the most civilized? Women's empowerment! Woman, how do you handle a man who always insists on his own way or a man who is just proud and arrogant?

Paul said, the whole law/commandment is summed up in one word – you shall love your neighbour as yourself (Galatians 5:14). Read this scripture carefully:

> *Owe no one anything except to love one another, for he who loves another has fulfilled the law. For the commandments, "You shall not commit adultery," "You shall not murder," "You shall not steal,"*

"You shall not bear false witness,"
"You shall not covet," and if there is
any other commandment, are all
summed up in this saying, namely,
<u>"You shall love your neighbor as
yourself."</u> Love does no harm to a
neighbor; therefore love is the
fulfillment of the law. And do this,
knowing the time, that now it is high
time to awake out of sleep; for now
our salvation is nearer than when we
first believed. The night is far spent,
the day is at hand. Therefore let us
cast off the works of darkness, and
let us put on the armor of light. Let
us walk properly, as in the day, not
in revelry and drunkenness, not in
lewdness and lust, not in strife and
envy. But put on the Lord Jesus
Christ, and make no provision for
the flesh, to fulfill its lusts.

Romans 13:8-14 (NKJV)

Paul concluded it all in first Corinthians
13:13 and said there are three forces that controls the

world – faith, hope, and love but the greatest of these is love.

Born Again?

"Beloved, let us love one another: for love is of God; and every one that loveth is born of God, and knoweth God"

1 John 4:7

Love is a definite sign of being born again. No one is truly born again and has no love. God is love, so you cannot carry the gene of God and not bear love. Jesus said, the only way people would know that you are my disciples is when you love one another. Love is the principal thing that distinguishes a believer from an unbeliever.

The whole first epistle of John is dedicated to preaching above loving one another. You cannot claim to know God and won't show love to the person next to you! The Bible rightly says in 1John 4:12 that "No man hath seen God at any time. If we love one another, God dwelleth in us, and his love is perfected in us."

The Bible says in Mark 16:17-18, that those who are born again, these signs shall follow them: "… shall they cast out devils; they shall speak with new tongues; they shall take up serpents; and if they drink any deadly thing, it shall not hurt them; they shall lay hands on the sick, and they shall recover." However, the Bible sharply contrast this in 1 Corinthians 13:1-3: "If I speak in the tongues of men and of angels, but have not love, I am a noisy gong or a clanging cymbal. And if I have prophetic powers, and understand all mysteries and all knowledge, and if I have all faith, so as to remove mountains, but have not love, I am nothing. If I give away all I have, and if I deliver my body to be burned, but have not love, I gain nothing." (RSV).

Love is everything. Love is light and the Bible says our lights must shine to the world. Wherever love is, the atmosphere of smiles and laughter is inevitable.

3

Two Categories
of Love

In Matt 22:36–39, two distinct categories of love was identified, that is:

Master, which is the great commandment in the law? Jesus said unto him, Thou shalt <u>love the Lord thy God</u> with all thy heart, and with all thy soul, and with all thy mind. This is the first and great commandment. And the second is like *unto it, Thou shalt <u>love thy neighbour</u> as thyself.*

Now, listen to this – the scripture says that every other law hangs on these laws (Matthew 22:40) – **the law of love for God** and **the law of love for your neighbour.** In other words, the love of God and mankind is the foundation of all other laws – biblical and worldly law. I know for the biblical law, we probably know how love is its foundation because the giver of those laws is Love (God) Himself. However, let me attempt to mention some few worldly laws and let's see how love is their foundation. Now, I believe the basic tenet of criminal, economic/business, civil rights, family or entertainment laws is to prevent or punish people who might cause a harmful or unfair treatment to others or their property.

Apostle Paul puts this so succinctly, in Romans 13:8-10:

"Let no debt remain outstanding, except the continuing debt to love one another, for whoever loves

others has fulfilled the law. The commandments, "you shall not commit adultery," "you shall not murder," "you shall not steal," "you shall not covet," and whatever other commandment there may be, are summed up in this one command: "Love your neighbour as yourself." Love does no harm to a neighbour. Therefore love is the fulfillment of the law."

Every law would have been rendered worthless if the law of love for your neighbour is fulfilled. Because love says what is good for you must be equally accorded your neighbour. Therefore, if something would be harmful or unfair to you, it is equally not good for your neighbour.

a) Love for God

The first supreme and greatest commandment to every man is to love God with everything man is made of – heart, soul, and mind (*spirit*). Love without love for God is no love at all.

Love has a meaning only if the love is from above. The reason why many have failed in the school of love is that their love is that of men. God is love and He has made us in His own image. Therefore, your first attraction should be to who you are – you are of God. Our first allegiance is to God – the creator before the created! Love for God is not a substitute for the love of anything else.

Three Expressions of Love for God[1]

- **Response to God and His Affairs**

A man's love for God is seen in the way he/she responds to God and His instructions. Jesus said in John 14:15 that "if ye love me, keep my commandments." I am sure by now you know that Jesus is God. See, Abraham obeyed God in two dramatic situations that do not make sense but it took his love for God. Abraham responded positively every time to God without questioning –

---

[1] This is taken from Bishop Solomon Adebayo, the founder and presiding Bishop of the Life Changer's International Church, Malawi, in his sermon on "Faith that Works by Love" on 14th May 2017

Abraham obeyed God's instruction to move out of his father's house to unknown place that God will show him later. Similarly, Abraham obeyed Go d to sacrifice his only loved son, Isaac, at a place God would later show him.

Tell me, if your partner always ignores your opinion on a matter would you consider that partner as loving? At least I have heard so many women complained that their men do not love them because they always ignore their opinion in a matter.

Your affection cannot be with God and your soul and mind (i.e. things that makes you happy e.g. money, friends, job) are somewhere else. Whatever you have or do must be dedicated and bring glory to God. In any case whatever we do is just a means to bring pleasure to God. On another note, we are just stewards and managers of God's property. The Bible says the earth and everything in it is the Lord's. Therefore, how well we manage God's property is a testament of our love for him.

David, in Psalm 132:4-5, said that he will not give sleep to his eyes or slumber to his eyelids until he finds a place for the LORD, a dwelling place for the Mighty God. David again said as the deer pants for the water brooks, so his heart pants for the Lord. David even though was not allowed by God to build His house, provided all that was necessary for the building of the house of the Lord. That is what the love for God makes a man to respond to the affairs of God.

- **Response to His Word**

Lovers often say "your wish is my command". God's word is His will for mankind. Jesus said a new commandment I give unto you i.e. to love God and love your neighbour as yourself. Again, He said if you love me you would keep my commandment. No one obeys the instructions of his/her enemy. Therefore, anyone who does not do the word of God is His enemy.

Similarly, our willingness to openly proclaim God and His agenda depicts our love for Him. You cannot claim to love someone and cannot talk about him/her to even your friends. Our being – speech and behaviour must speak of God. Jesus said if you love one another that is the only way the world would know that you are my disciples.

Our willingness to stand for things of God irrespective of the price is our show of love towards Him. The world must know the principles and virtues we stand for if we love Him – no compromising!

- **Giving & Sacrifice for God's Kingdom**

There is something so remarkable about Muslims – they are always willing to fight and die for the course of Allah. They will never accept blasphemy against their God. The Bible says where a man's treasure is there also his heart is. How important the things of God are to you determines how much you love Him.

Many believers are lovers of God in tongue only but not in deed. That is why the scripture above says love God with **all** your soul, heart and mind. Another scripture says love the Lord with your substance. David said I cannot give to my God what costs me nothing. You cannot cla im to love someone and cannot give him/her nothing. Our love for God must be demonstrated by our giving of ourselves and substances to Him. God Himself demonstrated this – the Bible says in John 3:16 that God loved the world so much that he gave His only son. 1 John 3:16 extends this to everyone – **"By this we know love,** because He laid down His life for us. And **we also ought to lay down our lives for the brethren**."

b) *Love for mankind*

The second supreme and greatest commandment is to love mankind – made likewise in the image of God. The Bible calls this the royal law and it says that **if you fulfill this, you have done well** (James 2:8). The Bible further says that we cannot say we love God who we cannot see and hate our brother that we can see. Let me show you something: interestingly, the love of God is incomplete without the love for

Mankind. We all know John 3:16 so well "For God so loved the world that he gave his only begotten Son ..." But look at what that love is:

> *Hereby perceive we the love of God, because he laid down his life for us: and we ought to lay down our lives for the brethren. But whoso hath this world's good, and seeth his brother have need, and shutteth up his bowels of compassion from him, how dwelleth the love of God in him? My little children, let us not love in word, neither in tongue; but in deed and in truth.*
>
> *1John 3:16-18*

Love of God is made of no effect without love for mankind. You cannot say you love God and not love the person next to you. The commandment goes further to say that "love your neighbour as yourself". Now tell me, who is your closest neighbour? Probably, your girl/boyfriend or your wife/husband! Can you then imagine rejecting yourself? Can you imagine you divorcing yourself?

Can you be separated from yourself? *That is how and why many of us have failed in the school of love*. Love is not selfish. Love your neighbour as yourself! As much as you cannot reject yourself no matter how bad you are, the same way, if you love your partner as yourself, you cannot reject/divorce him/her. Did you get this?

Now look at this:

> *My little children, let us not love in word, neither in tongue; but in deed and in truth.*
>
> *1John 3:18*

Four Kinds of Love

The scripture above reveals four kinds of love – (1) love in word, (2) love of the tongue, (3) love in deed, and (4) love in truth.

Love in Word and Love in Tongue

These two are fake loves – i.e. love in words and love in tongue. Interestingly these two are from the mouth and I say these take their source from Satan. These are deceptive loves. The Bible says Satan is the father of liars. Note, anytime anyone is let down in love, he/she is either deceived in words or by lying tongues. Many are victims of false love – the love of words and tongues. This has made many to fail in love. Love is not what you say or what you feel. Words and tongues would make you feel as loved but not loved at all. Love is **deeds**! Love is **truth**!

Love in Deed and Love in Truth

Love is what you do and not what you say. For God so loved the world that He **gave**, He did not **say** but did it. So we are also required to **do** – "lay down our lives for one another". Loving in deed means looking beyond your neighbour's weaknesses and shortcomings! You cannot love someone and cannot "for-give". Loving is giving! This is the God way of loving!

You don't love someone and deceive him. You tell him the truth – I was a prostitute, I have a short temper, etc. Even though you are ugly I still love you, even though you have a short temper, I still love you. That is the truth! Love does not conceal! Love changes not! Love is the truth! That is why the Bible says *"Love does not delight in evil but rejoices with the truth"*.

You would realise that all the characteristics of real love, as we would see in the previous chapter, fall under this kind of love – love in "deed" and love in "truth".

4

Who God is

In First John 4:8, the scriptures say that God is love. Now, I want you to close your mind for a moment on everything else you know God is but focus on just on this phrase "God is love". I want you to contrast this phrase with what the scriptures say in 1Corinthians 13:4-8 as below, and replace love with God:

> *"Love is patient, Love is kind. It does not envy, it does not boast, it is not proud. It is not rude, it is not self-seeking, it is not easily angered, it keeps no record of wrongs. Love*

does not delight in evil but rejoices with the truth. It always protects, always trusts, always hopes, always perseveres. Love never fails…"

This chapter may look repetitive to the preceding one but I want you to catch this revelation. I am not saying this is the only things God is but I want to draw your attention to this uniqueness of God as portrayed through the eyes of Love. If God is love, and love is all as above, then can you figure out who God is? That's is why it would take a deep search of the scriptures for you to truly know who God is. God is infinite. God is so GOOD that we often fail to recognize or understand. Here it is; replace all the 'Love' in the scriptures above with 'God' and it perfectly reveals who God is. Thus:

God is patient

You see why a thousand years is like a day to Him? In our local proverb, it is often said that if God wants to throw a stone at you, He does not throw it so quickly. Many people humorously say, "if He doesn't want to throw the stone, why is He holding it. God is so patient with everyone – the bad, the good. That is why, you would see an evil or wicked person who God knows and sees but He never kills him. If God was not patient, most of us would have received our punishments long time ago. It's in God's patience that we feel loved. Love/God is patient.

God is kind

Other words for kind are caring, thoughtful, benevolent, sympathetic, compassionate, nice, gentle, and generous. Do these words describe who you know God to be? Jesus was said to be moved with compassion so many times. That is who He is – He is compassionate. God is just kind. It takes a thoughtful person to love. If you think about the good things people do to you, you will express likewise to others. Nehemiah 9:17b says "… but thou art a God ready to pardon, gracious and merciful, slow to anger, **and of great kindness**, and forsakes them not."

God does not envy

The scriptures say that the earth and all that is in it is the Lord's. What does man have that God would envy him. He is all-in-all. The beginning and the end. Those who depends on Him or have faith in Him need not envy anybody. However note this, God is jealous. This jealousy is not a negative one but positive. As it is, every lover is jealous. If your man is not jealous positively about you, then his love is questionable!

God does not boast

If men were God, the world would have been ruled by autocrats. Men would have forced everybody against their wills. God is not comparable to any authority on earth. He is the "I am that I am" but He doesn't come down to show off like men do. God can do absolutely anything but He doesn't show off.

God is not proud

God wants to see His creations excelling and feel proud about them but He is not proud as to show off. The Bible described the presence of God to the Israelites in Exodus that the Israelites could not raise their heads to behold His presence. That is how great God is. He said the earth is His footstool and the heavens His seat thrown. But God is not full of Himself, walking around and ordering us to do what He wants. He allows all His creatures to express themselves. If God was full of pride, no one would even utter a word in his mouth that there is no God and live the next minute.

God is not rude

God is not impolite or ill-mannered. If He is, He would have appeared to you immediately at that point and place when you were engaged in that secret bad act. God would have exposed you that very minute when you were doing something so bad. Remember He is omnipresent. He is everywhere and sees everything that happens under the sun.

However, He will not intrude into your privacy. God is not an author of confusion. Our God is so gentle.

God is not self-seeking

Psalm 8:4 says what is man that God is so mindful of him? Who is man? It was God's sole decision to make man and make him in His image. God created the earth and place man on it and asked him to manage it and recreate it. Man is not the originator of anything. Man owns nothing on this earth, that is why when we leave this earth we leave with empty hands. Nevertheless, God has decided to give all to man. Our God, the owner of all things is willing to leave everything to us. Why then should you not be able to freely share. Love, God is not self-seeking, so you should not. God wants His glory but He wants your glory to show forth too.

God is not easily angered

So many scriptures (Nehemiah 9:17; Psalm 103:8; Psalms 145:8; Joel 2:13; Jonah 4:2; and Nahum 1:3) record that God is slow to anger. God knows every thought of man, so nothing surprises Him. God expects our flaws and weaknesses, so He is not easily angered when we fall. Love/God makes room for our flaws. That is why if any man/woman claims he/she loves you but cannot make room for your flaws, then it is no love at all. The only reason I am convinced that my wife loves me is because she has created a big room for all my flaws and shortcomings.

God keeps no record of wrongs

There is no god that is as forgiving as our God. He forgives our sins and remembers it no more. Now, if God were to record all our wrongs and remember them, can you imagine how great that would be and how unpardonable we would have stand? Even we ourselves cannot remember some of the wrongs we have done in the past. Love is so forgiving and forgiving the undeserved. That is why we say God is gracious. Grace means undeserved favour. Anyone who claims he/she loves you and keep on reminding you of your past mistakes or wrongs done to him/her, does not love you, period!

God does not delight in evil but rejoices with the truth

God is the truth. He sets the standards and so if He says it is wrong it is wrong. God is so pure so He can never condone the wrong. He is happy when we are right-eous. Many of us have failed in this respect, especially mothers. Many of us have erroneously have condoned wrongs on the basis of a so called love. That is not love at all. Love corrects. Many mothers have jumped into fights that their children wrongly started. No, don't do it, it doesn't show love! The Bible says that a man who loves his son corrects him; he does not condone the wrong. Love corrects in love.

God always protects

It is impossible to love something and not protect it. Wherever a man's treasure is, there his heart is. If you treasure love, your heart would be there. You see where most of us have failed as lovers? How can you be fighting the same thing you supposed to be defending? *Many of us fight our spouses as if they are our enemies.* Love MUST ALWAYS protect! God defends those who love Him. He protects them. David probably was the only one who enjoyed the most of this ministry of God. This scripture came so tellingly:

> *I have found David my servant; with my holy oil have I anointed him: With whom my hand shall be established: mine arm also shall strengthen him. The enemy shall not exact upon him; nor the son of wickedness afflict him. And I will beat down his foes before his face, and plague them that hate him.*
>
> *Psalms 89:20-23*

This is what love does. Several scriptures tell us how God protects His loved ones. No one protects or defend his own like God. The nature of God, being love, puts Him on urge whenever His people are suffering, unless it is for a lesson. Love protects!

God always trusts and hopes

The Bible says even when we were yet still sinners Christ died for us. The parable of the prodigal son was an epitome of God's trusts and hopes towards transgressors. God is always trusting and hoping that we will change our ways and return to Him. That is why no other religion has the word "repentance" like Christianity. This should be the attitude of everyone who calls him/herself a lover. We must always trust and have hope for our spouses to change, to put up the right behaviour and attitude. That is why the last two attitudes of God below are so crucial.

God always perseveres

God never give up on people. God is always hoping and trusting that we will have a change of heart. Imagine if God was man, He would have given up on this world long time ago, but God perseveres.

God endures our insolence and disobedience. Our lover never gives up on us no matter horrible we are. He still loves us and endures our shortcomings. If God can take all your weaknesses, why is it so difficult for you to bear with your spouse's meager weakness? It is time we persevere in love and not faint so quickly. The extent and rate of divorce is so high because men and women alike are so selfish and unwilling to endure the storms of love affair. Note that there is a master anti-marriage, the devil himself. So don't take it so lightly anytime you face a challenge in your relationship. It could be the devil and its cohorts at work. Endure it and victory will be yours in Jesus name!

Second Peter 3:9 say "the Lord is not slack concerning his promise, as some men count slackness; but is longsuffering to us-ward, not willing that any should perish, but that all should come to repentance." God perseveres due to his love towards us.

God never fails

Above all God cannot and will never fail. True love never fails. It's only fake love that fails. You see why many of us have failed in our so-called "love affair" at one point? It is very few who have succeeded in maintaining their relationship no matter the storm. Many parents disown their children due to some minor unhealthy conducts. Love never fails. Our God never fail in love, so we cannot fail either! True lovers stick forever.

5

Love, a Conqueror

*"Hatred does not conquer hatred
BUT LOVE conquers hatred"*

Wherever love is, it conquers. No one truly conquers life without love. Even fear is conquered in love. Everything under the sun is conquerable with love. In any case, love is God, the almighty Himself, so who can stand Him? Anytime you put on love, you put on God Himself. Anytime you show love, you are showing your father's true gene. Why is it possible for man and wild animals e.g. a lion or snake, to live together? Wild beasts are tamed by love. If you love something you will have patience for it.

> *"Nay, in all these things we are more than conquerors through him that <u>loved</u> us"*
>
> *Romans 8:37*

The forces in this world make many people unfaithful. It is so difficult for people who started being unfaithful to stop. However, there is a stronger force that is able to stop it – i.e. love! The Bible says God is love – in reverse, we can say love is God. If there is nothing which is impossible for God, then there is nothing that love cannot do or overcome. That is why the first question or query that comes into the mind of any victim of unfaithful partner is whether the partner loves him/her. Any man/woman who divine love is working in him/her would not be unfaithful to the partner. Unfaithfulness is a sign that God is not with a man. Therefore, it would take love to restore an unfaithful partner. Look at this:

Brethren, if a man be overtaken in a fault, ye which are spiritual, restore such an one in the spirit of meekness; considering thyself, lest thou also be tempted.

Galatians 6:1

Now, according to this scripture above, it would take "those who are spiritual" to restore any man who is overtaken in a fault. We can safely say that love is equal to being spiritual. This is because the Bible also says God is spirit – so if God is love and He is also spirit – then we can say love is equal to being spiritual. Actually, the Bible in Basic English (BBE) version rendered the phrase "spirit of meekness" as "spirit of love". It takes the spirit of love to restore a believer who has sinned or backslided. The spirit of love is what covers people's multitude of sin, shortcomings and flaws. Watch it; those who feel so spiritual and fail to observe the later part of the above scripture above gets caught up in their own faults too.

Many, particularly believers, have caused their relationships or marriages to fail because they have not applied the law of love. Many parents have driven their children into bad companies or into the arm of the devil because they fail to correct their children in love. It takes applying all the characteristics in 1 Corinthians 13:4-8 to be able to conquer anyone overtaken by wrongdoing. This is the law Jesus applied to the woman caught in adultery in John 8. You see, the Mosaic Law says if a woman is caught in adultery, she should be stoned. However, Jesus says that my new COMMANDMENT (law) is **the law of love**. It can only take the spirit of love (God) for a woman whose husband has cheated on her to forgive him. It would only take love or the intervention of God (love) for a man to forgive his wife caught in adultery.

Please understand this; anyone overtaken in wrongdoing have had his/her heart captured by the devil. Therefore, it will not take flesh and human wisdom to rescue him but God (love). That is why I don't believe in a 'fire-for-fire' approach in dispute settlement or correcting people through unwise rebukes. I believe that even our children should be corrected in love. If your child deserve punishment, let him or her understand you are doing it because you love him/her so that he/she doesn't end up a liability in life or die prematurely according to the scriptures of those who don't obey their parents.

People in disagreement or in sin have their hearts already taken by the devil. Any unwise intervention, which is not divinely led just make such situations or individuals worse. You know why most of us get into disagreements over minor issues; we just fail to correct each other in love. You know what; I have been there so I know how it feels. Look, many people have committed suicide because those around them have failed to rescue them from the devil through love. Rather, unfortunately they presented themselves as instruments in self-righteousness clothes, as the Pharisees do, to condemn such wrongdoers and stone them by their acts to Satan or death.

Look at this scenario with Jesus again:

And it happened in the fulfilling of the days of His taking up, He steadfastly set His face to go to Jerusalem. And He sent messengers before His face. And they went and entered into a village of the Samaritans to make ready for Him. And they did not receive Him, because His face was going toward Jerusalem. And seeing, His disciples James and John said, Lord, do You desire that we command fire to come down from Heaven and consume them, even as Elijah did? But He turned and rebuked them and said, <u>You do not know of what spirit you are</u>. For the Son of man has not come to destroy men's lives, but to save. And they went to another village.

(Luke 9:51-56; MKJV)

Wow, we are of love. Look at the way He put it "you do not know what spirit you are". We are spirit of God – LOVE. Love does not recompense wrong with wrong. Love is a substitute for punishment. John and James said, Master, for the sin of this people let us call down fire from Heaven to consume them. However, Jesus says who we are, Love, does not allow us to pay evil for evil. Oh yes, see, God loved us when we were yet sinners (Romans 5:8). "Herein is love, not that we loved God, but that he loved us, and sent his Son to be the propitiation for our sins. Beloved, if God so loved us, we ought also to love one another." (1Jo 4:10-11)

Now let's look at this subject in other fields, not just in a relationships or marriages. It would only take God (love) to change someone who is unfaithful in business or finance. The Bible says love is not self-seeking. Every unfaithfulness is a result of a self-ish desire. The Bible says in 2 Corinthians 5:4 that "… the love of Christ constrains us…" Love controls. Love is an inside force that makes a man to say no to anything that is wrong, no matter how tempting or juicy it is.

There is a saying that a man who is down fears no fall. Anyone who tastes unfaithfulness remains there – he just continues in it. He/she just cannot stop. That is why it takes serious intersession and expression of love to rescue an unfaithful person. No amount of quarrels or putting right or revenge would bring him/her back. It would take only the indomitable and unfailing love to bring him/her back. Love never fails!

You see, when I started writing this book I never knew I was writing it about myself even though clearly I have failed in some of the marking schemes of 1 Corinthians 13. Later on, an experience in my life caught my attention – I have totally failed in love. My wife on the other hand has demonstrated absolute love towards me. I was unfaithful to my wife but SHE FORGAVE me! Love forgives and keeps no records of wrongs done to her. This has rescued me. If not I would have continued in the path of unfaithfulness. I was selfish and not kind to my wife. I saw God's hand in my drama. He orchestrated a scheme that was in the mind of my partner of unfaithfulness meant for my destruction but it turned for my redemption. It turned to me for a testimony! My wife truly conquered my heart now!

6

Love and War

God's law concerning life is summarized in one word, "love". Just think about it, every law under the sun can be placed in the box of the characteristics of love. Be it criminal, civil or economic law. Look at this, love does not envy, love is not self-seeking, and love does not delight in evil. ". Love does no harm to a neighbour. What drives crime? Envy, selfishness and evil are undoubtedly reasons for crime. What about unfair economic competition or trade practices? I guess you understand what I mean by now. The Bible rightly put it this way:

"For all the law is fulfilled in one word, even in this: "You shall love your neighbor as yourself."

Galatians 5:14 (NKJV)

"For the commandments, "You shall not commit adultery," "You shall not murder," "You shall not steal," "You shall not bear false witness," "You shall not covet, " and if there is any other commandment, are all summed up in this saying, namely, "You shall love your neighbor as yourself". Love does no harm to a neighbor; therefore love is the fulfillment of the law.

Romans 13:9-10 (NKJV)

Love does no harm to her neighbour; therefore love is the fulfillment of the law. Imagine if everyone would believe that his/her neighbour is as just good as him, how we would have not seen politicians killing others for the sake of retaining power. Imagine if all 'extremist' Muslims would just but love – love does not think of himself highly than others and love is not self-seeking – the world would not be spending so much in cash and man-hours trying to stop innocent killings all in the name of a belief.

> *"And above all things have fervent love for one another, for "love will cover a multitude of sins.""*

> *1Peter 4:8 (NKJV)*

Jesus called it the royal law (James 2:8). This is the law that is from above, not manipulated by pretense, emotion, pressure, politics or ideology. It is divine. I believe that if everyone should have this kind of love, the world would cease to have strife and wars that we see all around us. Let's see some of my thoughts on this below.

Adultery and War

Remember this: love always protects? One of the protective instincts of love is to fight for what is rightfully his. Many houses have turned into battlegrounds as a result of adultery. In villages, one village can go to war because another man or woman is flirting with another man's wife or husband. Simply, adultery could ignite war among people.

Murder and War

Murder has often caused people to go to war. I understand that anytime a Palestinian kill one Israelis, Israel wages war on Palestinians to take more lives. The taking of life for whatever reason is not acceptable to even God, and for that matter human beings. Many people and tribes will go all the way out to revenge their loved ones.

Stealing and War

Undoubtedly, the many wars we have around the world today are a result of a claim of theft. Most of them surround the unrightful claim of ownership of land. The unending war between Israel and Palestine is due to a dispute over a piece of land. Most probably, one of them is trying to steal from the other. In almost every country, one tribe or village is disputing a land or property. Companies often go to legal wars over theft of copyright or company secret. Unfortunately, the church has not been spared. Many Pastors and members are at war over a church property or membership. Taking unrightfully what does not belong to you will always be met with a strong defense that often results in war.

Bearing false witness and War

Many tribes and countries have been misled into war because someone had refused to tell the truth. Some marriages and families are at war because someone had concealed the truth and bore a false witness. Dishonest wickedness is the bane of the destruction of our society. Political parties are at longer heads because none of them is not willing to uphold the truth. Satan is the father of liars and his goal is to steal people's joy and peace, kill and destroy people. Bearing false witness is one of Satan's dangerous weapons to destroy the fabric of our society. It is from the dark world. However, the good news is this: the Bible says that darkness cannot comprehend light. God is light and He is love. Love is light, therefore, conquer darkness with your love. If all can love to the point that we feel the pain we would put someone through by falsely bearing witness against him/her, the world would be filled with love.

Covetousness and War

Greed has led many to war. It is in men, in villages, in cities, in nations, and unfortunately in Pastors and churches. Due to greed, people would be willing to go to war for a piece of land. An individual or group of individuals do not mind to sacrifice the future of their children or generations just for their own self-aggrandizement. Greed leads a man to kill his child or wife for money. Another word for covetousness is materialism. The world today is so full of people who do not care about who is hurting or in need. All they want is to have possessions; possessions they would soon die and leave behind. It is so pathetic the way some human beings hoard possessions that they are unable to spend even one thousands of during their lifetime. Craving for material things has been the main driving force behind every thought of men these days. No one is willing to show love through sharing. It is time for people who are called of God to show the way, the way of love. Love is kind and not self-seeking.

7

Love and Marriage

First Corinthians 13:13 say that faith, hope and love abides but the greatest of these is love. That means love is the most essential virtue in all lives endeavours. In any case, love is God, the Almighty Himself. Therefore, it must be the greatest. However, love is not the first requirement for marriage. I agree love is the greatest but love must not be your first consideration when you choose your life partner. It is a complete myth and the cause of many heartbreaks and marriage failures. Love, as strong as it is, particularly relational love, is not and must not be the first priority in choosing your life partner.

There is something stronger than relational love. That is why lovers all over the world are failing to stick together. The truth is this; love never fails! Therefore, if love should be the main factor to get married, then, marriage or relationships should not fail because love never fails. Why then do we see so many marriages or relationships failing? It is not because love was not there or God (love) was not there. There is something missing! That thing is PURPOSE! You see, the creator of marriage or relationship is God. Although, the primary reason God created man is love or fellowship, this is not the same reason God created marriage. I want you to take your time to read carefully the scripture below:

> *And the LORD God took the man, and put him into the garden of Eden to dress it and to keep it... And the LORD God said, It is not good that the man should be alone; I will make him an help meet for him. And out of*

the ground the LORD God formed every beast of the field, and every fowl of the air; and brought them unto Adam to see what he would call them: and whatsoever Adam called every living creature, that was the name thereof. And Adam gave names to all cattle, and to the fowl of the air, and to every beast of the field; but for Adam there was not found an help meet for him. And the LORD God caused a deep sleep to fall upon Adam, and he slept: and he took one of his ribs, and closed up the flesh instead thereof; And the rib, which the LORD God had taken from man, made he a woman, and brought her unto the man. And Adam said, This is now bone of my bones, and flesh of my flesh: she shall be called Woman, because she was taken out of Man. Therefore, shall a man leave his father and his mother, and shall cleave unto his wife: and they shall be one flesh.

*And they were both naked, the man
and his wife, and were not ashamed.*

(Genesis 2:15-25)

This was the beginning of marriage. Now,
can you tell me the place of love in the institution of
marriage here? Dr. Munroe said when the purpose
of a thin is not known abuse is inevitable. Can you
also figure out the purpose of marriage from the
scripture above? Why did God created the woman?
Is it for loving the man? NO! God say it is not good
for the man to be ALONE. Now, understand this:
this does not mean the man was lonely. Being alone
does not mean loneliness. What is the man alone
doing? "… the LORD God took the man, and put
him into the garden of Eden **to dress it and to keep
it**" Basically, God said **it is not good for the man
alone to be keeping and dressing this garden**, so I
will create for him a **HELP** meet. Marriage is a
partnership, that is why we call the couples partners.
Are they partners in love? No! They are partners in
God's assignment for the man.

The reason why many relationships and marriages are failing is due to lack of understanding of this institution called marriage. Many have erroneously gotten married because of love. Then immediately they realised that love alone cannot keep them together. You see, the Bible says that how can two people stay together unless they are in agreement. This is purpose! If you and your wife does not have a common purpose then you are not in agreement and according to that scripture, you cannot stay together.

Another part of this problem is this. According to the scripture above, man was given the assignment of keeping and dressing the garden before the woman was brought to help him. This is the problem in today's marriages. Many men have not yet discovered their purpose or assignment before getting married. Therefore, their wives (helpers) get to them with nothing to help with. Now, I am not talking about a job here. Credit to Dr. Myles Munroe, there is a difference between a job and work. A job is what you are paid to do. A work is what you are born to do or become. You can be fired or retired from your job but you can't be fired or retired from your work. Your work is your divine assignment or purpose on earth and so it came with you equipped with gift(s) or talent(s) to do it. That is why you can't be fired from it. It is entirely attached to your gifts and skills.

Many men are confused or better still, are trying to figure out what they are on earth to do. They therefore leave their wives with no choice but **"to look for something to do"**. The Bible say the devil finds work for an idle hands. This time it is not the devil but many women themselves have to find something for their idle hands. Oh, I heard so many women say this: "I have to look for something to do". At least I have heard my wife said this several times. Why? They cannot see what their men are doing that they can help. This is the truth is this: in most cases when women leave their men to look for something better to do, love was still there. In other words, where marriages fail, love was still present. That is why, in relationships or marriages where the man is not doing any meaningful work, the woman most often bound to leave. Purpose gives people joy. It keeps them alive.

Now, does this mean that love has no place in marriage? NO, God forbid! Most part of this book categorically emphasized the role of love in relationships and marriages. However, the place of love is in achieving purpose. That is why all the attributes of love in 1Corinthians 13 have elements of work. The virtues of love guarantees success. It will take love for you to exercise patience and trust for the fulfilment of your assignment. Love must lead you to accomplishments. Love is a doer. Actually, love is what we are. Love grows in its proper environment. God (love) is not a purposeless God but a purposeful God. Love thrives with purpose.

8

Grace to Love

And now these three remain: faith, hope and love. But the greatest of these is LOVE"

1Corinthians 13:13

The Bible says nothing is given unto any man unless it comes from above. I believe it takes the grace of God to be able to love because some people are just unlovable. As I said in some pages of this book, love is giving and giving to the undeserving. That is why Jesus said we should love even your enemies. However, this is only possible with grace. Everybody must make it a daily habit to ask God for grace to love because everyday situations will test your love. Many times when I really resolved to love my wife, those are the times that my love is most tested. I will be honest with you I most often fail. Most of us have failed in the school of love!

From the scriptures above, it is not your faith that is the greatest but love. So choose Love! The world would be a better place for us if you choose to love. Note, God created us in His own image and the Bible says God is Love. However, disobedience of men brought the world this far. This is for sure: we would NOT see the end of wars: wives against husbands, father against children or children against parents, tribes against tribes, nations against nations. However, those who will choose to go back to God's supreme command to **love their neighbours as themselves** will enjoy peace in the midst of the storms and chaos of this world.

Why We Must Love

Love is a command (Mt 22:37-40)

Love is not negotiable. It is required of everyman to love God, first, and love all including our enemies. God commands it, period!

Love edifies or builds up one another (1 Cor 8:1)

The Bible says if anyone is overtaken in sin, those who are spiritual should restore him in love. Love is a builder and it improves people and does not destroy. I have heard so many times about men who cheat on their wives change due to the love their wives show them instead of revenge.

Love is an identity (John 13:35)

Jesus said, the only way people will know that you are my disciples is when you love one another. God is love and those who are born of him must bear the surname of love.

Love is salvation (Matt 19:16, 19; Luke 10:25-27)

Jesus was asked at two separate times, how one could enter into eternal life and He did not miss words at all. Love is a requirement for entering into the kingdom of God. To be adopted into the kingdom of God, you must adopt and act His name, love.

Love makes us dwell in God (Ps 69:36) and hence protection

Love (God) protects his loved ones (Ps 97:10; John 14:15-16). Anytime we love, we open God's bosom to our protection. As I said before, light and darkness cannot mix, therefore love and hatred cannot stay together. Anytime we are in love with God and our neighbours, we dwell in God's protective arms.

We receive mercy via love (Ps 119:132)

God always shows mercy to all those who loved him. Naturally, we all show mercy to those we love. That's why the scriptures say that love covers multitude of sin. God expects us to demonstrate our love through being merciful to others as He does unto us.

Life is summed up in Love (Rom 13:9)

Everything in life can successfully be done through the virtue/ attitude of love. Everything that is unacceptable in life is an attitude contrary to the virtue of love. Love makes life more meaningful. Even worldly love makes people want to stick together.

So that you will be relevant in the body of Christ (1 Cor 13:1-3)

Do not be a "sounding brass or a clanging cymbal"! Our relevance in the kingdom of God is neither in speaking tongues, having prophetic powers, understanding mysteries or in well doing. It all comes down to love! The Bible says if we do well to those who do well to us, how different are we from unbelievers. Love is wider and deeper than all the above. Again, remember Jesus said this is our identity, if we love one another.

It shows that the Holy Spirit dwells in us (Gal 5:22)

Love is a fruit of the Holy Spirit. One sure way we can know whether the Holy Spirit is in you or not is your fruit of love or hatred. Unforgiving people are unmistakably Holy Spirit void people.

God fulfills his covenant through love (Daniel 9:4)

God said those who reject Him, He is likely to reject them. Daniel said God keeps his covenant with those who love him and this is true of every father. God's love for us constraints Him to fulfill His covenant to us. In any case, our covenant with Him was founded on His love. God so loved the world that He gave His only begotten son that whosoever believes in Him should not perish but have everlasting life. The covenant of everlasting life and its accompanied benefits are only fulfilled through love.

Coming Soon...

1. After Salvation, WHAT?

2. Why Ladies Make the Same Mistakes their Mothers Made

3. Would You Still Serve Him

4. STEWARDship PARENTing

www.ingramcontent.com/pod-product-compliance
Lightning Source LLC
Chambersburg PA
CBHW021208020426
42331CB00003B/254